NATIONAL GEOGRAPHIC
School Publishing

D0503785

Contar

Tessa Patel

PICTURE CREDITS
Illustrations by Jeff Lang (4–5, 14–15).
Cover, 1, 7 (below), 8 (below left & below right), 9 (below right), 10 (all), 12 (above left, above right & below left), Photolibrary.com; 2, 6 (right), 8 (background & above right), 9 (background), 11 (all), 12 (below right), APL/Corbis; 6 (above left), Richard Naude/Alamy; 6 (background), 7 (background), Photodisc; 7 (above), Ibis for Kids Australia; 9 (above left), Getty Images; 10 (background), 11 (background), Digital Vision; 12 (background), 13 (background), Image Source.

Produced through the worldwide resources of the National Geographic Society, John M. Fahey, Jr., President and Chief Executive Officer; Gilbert M. Grosvenor, Chairman of the Board.

PREPARED BY NATIONAL GEOGRAPHIC SCHOOL PUBLISHING
Ericka Markman, Senior Vice President and President Children's Books and Education Publishing Group; Steve Mico, Senior Vice President and Publisher; Marianne Hiland, Editorial Director; Lynnette Brent, Executive Editor; Michael Murphy and Barbara Wood, Senior Editors; Bea Jackson, Design Director; David Dumo, Art Director; Margaret Sidlowsky, Illustrations Director; Matt Wascavage, Manager of Publishing Services; Sean Philpotts, Production Manager.

SPANISH LANGUAGE VERSION PREPARED BY NATIONAL GEOGRAPHIC SCHOOL PUBLISHING GROUP
Sheron Long, CEO; Sam Gesumaria, President; Fran Downey, Vice President and Publisher; Margaret Sidlosky, Director of Design and Illustrations; Paul Osborn, Senior Editor; Sean Philpotts, Project Manager; Lisa Pergolizzi, Production Manager.

MANUFACTURING AND QUALITY MANAGEMENT
Christopher A. Liedel, Chief Financial Officer; George Bounelis, Vice President; Clifton M. Brown III, Director.

BOOK DEVELOPMENT
Ibis for Kids Australia Pty Limited.

SPANISH LANGUAGE TRANSLATION
Tatiana Acosta/Guillermo Gutiérrez

SPANISH LANGUAGE BOOK DEVELOPMENT
Navta Associates, Inc.

Published by the National Geographic Society
Washington, D.C. 20036-4688

Copyright © 2008 National Geographic Society. All rights reserved.
Reproduction of the whole or any part of the contents without written permission from the publisher is prohibited. National Geographic, National Geographic School Publishing, National Geographic Windows on Literacy and the Yellow Border are registered trademarks of the National Geographic Society.

ISBN: 978-0-7362-3834-2

Printed in the U.S.A.

19 18 17 16 15 14

10 9 8 7 6 5 4 3

Contenido

Pensar y conversar	4
Contar en una merienda	6
Contar en una charca	8
Contar en un jardín	10
Hacer una gráfica	12
Usar lo que aprendieron	14
Glosario ilustrado	16

Pensar y conversar

¿Cuántas personas hay en el parque? ¿Qué otras cosas podemos contar?

Contar en una merienda

Podemos contar cosas en una merienda. Contemos lo que hay en cada fotografía.

sándwiches
cerezas

Contar en una charca

Podemos contar cosas en una charca.
Contemos lo que hay en cada fotografía.

ranas
patitos
piedras

Contar en un jardín

Podemos contar cosas en un jardín.
Contemos lo que hay en cada fotografía.

hormigas
flores amarillas
abejas

Hacer una gráfica

Para mostrar cuántas cosas contamos, podemos hacer una gráfica.

¿Cuántos hay?

10				
9				
8				
7				
6				
5				
4				
3				
2				
1				
	patitos	pájaros	peces	abejas

Usar lo que aprendieron

¿Cuántas barcas hay en el lago? ¿Qué más podemos contar?

cero
uno
dos
tres
cuatro
cinco
seis
siete
ocho
nueve
diez

Glosario ilustrado

0 cero	
1 uno	
2 dos	
3 tres	
4 cuatro	
5 cinco	
6 seis	
7 siete	
8 ocho	
9 nueve	
10 diez